To:

_____

From:

_____

Date:

_____

My heart rejoices and I'm thankful, too,
That I could share this book with you,
For all my poems are woven of
Words I borrow from our Father above ...

On the wings of Prayer

the morning I lay my requests before you and wait in expectation. In the morning, O Lord, you hear my voice; in

HELEN STEINER RICE

Christian Art Gifts

On the wings of prayer contains excerpts from
A book of prayer, first published by Fleming
H. Revell, a division of Baker Book House Company,
PO Box 6287, Grand Rapids, MI 49516-6287

© 1995 by Virginia J. Ruehlmann and
The Helen Steiner Rice Foundation
Compiled by Virginia J. Ruehlmann

First edition published in South Africa by Christian Art Publishers
PO Box 1599, Vereeniging, 1930
© 1996

Second edition © 2000 by Christian Art Gifts

Cover designed by Christian Art Gifts

Printed and bound in Hong Kong

ISBN 1-86852-605-4

00 01 02 03 04 05 06 07 08 09 - 10 9 8 7 6 5 4 3 2 1

Contents

The Helen Steiner Rice Foundation

The Helen Steiner Rice Foundation

God knows no strangers, He loves us all,
The poor, the rich, the great, the small.
He is a Friend who is always there
To share our troubles and lessen our care.
No one is a stranger in God's sight,
For God is love and in His Light
May we, too, try in our small way
To make new friends from day to day.

Whatever the celebration, whatever the day, whatever the event, whatever the occasion, Helen Steiner Rice possessed the ability to express the appropriate feeling for that particular moment in time.

A happening became happier, a sentiment more sentimental, a memory more memorable because of her deep sensitivity to put into understandable language the emotion being experienced. Her positive attitude, her concern for others, and her love of God are identifiable threads woven into her life, her work ... and even her death.

Prior to her passing, she established the

Helen Steiner Rice Foundation, a nonprofit corporation whose purpose is to award grants to worthy charitable programs that aid the elderly, the needy, and the poor. In her lifetime, these were the individuals about whom Mrs. Rice was greatly concerned.

Royalties from the sale of this book will add to the financial capabilities of the *Helen Steiner Rice Foundation*, thus making possible additional grants to various qualified, worthwhile, and charitable programs. Because of her foresight, her caring, and her deep convictions, Helen Steiner Rice continues to touch a countless number of lives. Thank you for your assistance in helping to keep Helen's dream alive.

Virginia J. Ruehlmann, Administrator
The Helen Steiner Rice Foundation
Suite 2100, Atrium Two
221 E. Fourth Street
Cincinnati, Ohio 45201

Introduction

Prayer is a magnificent and generous gift from our Father. It is also a conversation, a relationship, a communication with God, initiated by the individual or group doing the praying. Prayer can be

silent or audible,
spontaneous or formal,
memorized or extemporaneous,
expressed privately or
with other members of a family,
church, or organization,
said or sung in a secluded location,
or walking on a crowded street,
while driving or riding in a car, dining or
drifting off to sleep.

Anytime and anywhere is a place for prayer.
A prayer can be a form of adoration or praise,

an expression of love and loyalty,
appreciation and thanksgiving,
celebration or consolation, a petition,
a statement of contrition,
a plea for forgiveness or a request for guidance.

Prayers can be simply or elaborately stated.

The important characteristics include
the qualities of humility, fidelity, faith,

trust, and sincerity.
Simple, direct, and honest supplications
are heard as clearly
as loquacious and embellished pontifications.
There are no boundaries as to what to pray
for –
one should feel free to take everything
to God in prayer.
The challenge is not only in taking
a concern to Him but
trusting in God's answer and the timing
of His response.
Prayer offers a renewal and revitalization of
spirit and hope.
It is not as important to physically kneel
in prayer but rather to have one's spirit
bow in an attitude of respect.
One's prayer life should be an ongoing process,
continuing to become ever more meaningful,
ever more helpful, as
it progresses onward toward the eternal
goal.
Helen Steiner Rice knew the value of a
consistent prayerful life and expressed such in
many of her poems. May this collection assist
you in developing and following your own
prayer life.

Prayerfully,
–Virginia J. Ruehlmann –

Daily prayers

Give us today our daily bread.

~ Matthew 6:11 NAB ~

Should a person pray daily? Absolutely! Daily! Nightly! Frequently throughout the day. Praying daily strengthens a person, brightens the day, lightens the cares, relieves one's tension, and increases the quietude of one's soul.

The personal prayer of the author

Bless us, heavenly Father –
forgive our erring ways.
Grant us strength to serve Thee,
put purpose in our days.
Give us understanding,
enough to make us kind,
So we may judge all people
with our hearts and not our minds.
And teach us to be patient
in everything we do,
Content to trust Your wisdom
and to follow after You …
And help us when we falter
and hear us when we pray,
And receive us in Thy kingdom
to dwell with Thee some day.
This is the prayer that I faithfully say
to help me meet the new dawning day,
For I never could meet life's daily demands
unless I was sure He was holding my hand.
And priceless indeed would be my reward
to know that you shared my prayer to the Lord.

*My strength and courage is the
LORD and he has been my savior.*

~ Psalm 118:14 NAB ~

Good morning, God!

You are ushering in another day,
untouched and freshly new,
So here I am to ask You, God,
if You'll renew me, too.
Forgive the many errors
that I made yesterday
And let me try again, dear God,
to walk closer in Thy way.
But, Father, I am well aware
I can't make it on my own,
So take my hand and hold it tight,
for I can't walk alone.

*Create in me a pure heart, O God,
and renew a steadfast spirit within me.*

~ Psalm 51:10 NIV ~

My daily prayer

God, be my resting place and my protection
In hours of trouble, defeat and dejection.
May I never give way to self-pity and sorrow,
May I always be sure of a better tomorrow,
May I stand undaunted, come what may,
Secure in the knowledge I have only to pray
And ask my Creator and Father above
To keep me serene in His grace and His love!

He who fears the Lord has
a secure fortress, and for
his children it will be a refuge.

~ Proverbs 14:26 NIV ~

Daily prayers
dissolve your cares

I meet God in the morning
and go with Him through the day,
Then in the stillness of the night
before sleep comes I pray
That God will just take over
all the problems I couldn't solve,
And in the peacefulness of sleep
my cares will all dissolve.
So when I open up my eyes
to greet another day,
I'll find myself renewed in strength
and there will open up a way
To meet what seemed impossible
for me to solve alone,
And once again I'll be assured
I am never on my own.
For if we try to stand alone
we are weak and we will fall,
For God is always greatest
when we're helpless, lost and small.
And no day is unmeetable
if, on rising, our first thought
Is to thank God for the blessings

that His loving care has brought.
For there can be no failures
or hopeless, unsaved sinners
If we enlist the help of God,
who makes all losers winners.
So meet Him in the morning
and go with Him through the day,
And thank Him for His guidance
each evening when you pray –
And if you follow faithfully
this daily way to pray,
You will never in your lifetime
face another hopeless day.

*My eyes are awake before the
watches of the night, that I may
meditate upon thy promise.*

~ Psalm 119:148 RSV ~

It's me again, God

Remember me, God!
I come every day
Just to talk with You, Lord,
and to learn how to pray.
You make me feel welcome,
You reach out Your hand.
I need never explain,
for You understand.
I come to You frightened
and burdened with care,
So lonely and lost
and so filled with despair,
And suddenly, Lord,
I'm no longer afraid –
My burden is lighter
and the dark shadows fade.
Oh God, what a comfort
to know that You care
And to know when I seek You,
You will always be there.

Today's prayer

Teach me to give of myself
in whatever way I can,
of whatever I have to give.

Teach me to value myself –
my time, my talents,
my purpose, my life,
my meaning in Your world.

> *Guide me in your truth and teach
> me; for you are God my Savior.*
>
> ~ Psalm 25:5 NIV ~

The first thing every morning and the last thing every night

Were you too busy this morning
to quietly stop and pray?
Did you hurry and drink your coffee
then frantically rush away,
Consoling yourself by saying –
God will always be there
Waiting to hear my petitions
ready to answer each prayer?
It's true that the great, generous Savior
forgives our transgressions each day
And patiently waits for lost sheep
who constantly seem to stray,
But moments of prayer once omitted
in the busy rush of the day
Can never again be recaptured,
for they silently slip away.
And no one regains that blessing
that would have been theirs if they'd prayed,
For blessings are lost forever
in prayers that are often delayed.
And strength is gained in the morning

to endure the trials of the day
When we visit with God in person
in a quiet and unhurried way,
For only through prayer that's unhurried
can the needs of the day be met
And only in prayers said at evening
can we sleep without fears or regret –
For all of our errors and failures
that we made in the course of the day
Are freely forgiven at nighttime
when we kneel down and earnestly pray.
So seek the Lord in the morning
and never forget Him at night,
For prayer is an unfailing blessing
that makes every burden seem light.

*In the morning, O Lord, you hear my
voice; in the morning I lay my requests
before you and wait in expectation.*

~ Psalm 5:3 NIV ~

Patience
through prayer

Love is patient, love is kind.

1 Corinthians 13:4 NAB

It is difficult to suffer uncomplainingly and to bear up under stress when one endures difficult circumstances, insults, or actions. To do this requires the gifts of faith and patience. But the rewards for doing so are contentment and peace. Through prayer we learn to accept life's difficulties with patience.

A prayer for patience

God, teach me to be patient,
teach me to go slow —
Teach me how to wait on You
when my way I do not know.
Teach me sweet forbearance
when things do not go right
So I remain unruffled
when others grow uptight.
Teach me how to quiet
my racing, rising heart
So I might hear the answer
You are trying to impart.
Teach me to let go, dear God,
and pray undisturbed until
My heart is filled with inner peace
and I learn to know Your will.

Be still before the Lord,
and wait patiently for him.

~ Psalm 37:7 RSV ~

People's problems

Everyone has problems in this restless world of care,
Everyone grows weary with the cross they have to bear.
Everyone is troubled and their skies are overcast
As they try to face the future while dwelling in the past.
But people with their problems only listen with one ear,
For people only listen to the things they want to hear,
And only hear the kind of things they're able to believe,
Answers that God gives them they're not ready to receive.

So while the people's problems keep growing every day
And they still try to solve them in their ever willful way,
God seeks to help, and watches, waiting always patiently
To help them solve their problems, whatever they may be.

And he said to all, "If any man would come after me, let him deny himself and take up his cross daily and follow me."

~ Luke 9:23 RSV ~

Perseverance

Oh Lord, don't let me falter
don't let me lose my way.
Don't let me cease to carry
my burden, day by day.
Oh Lord, don't let me stumble –
don't let me fall and quit,
Help me to find my task
and help me shoulder it.

You, dear children are from God and have overcome them, because the one who is in you is greater than the one who is in the world.

~ 1 John 4:4 NIV ~

Give me the contentment of acceptance

In the deep, dark hours of my distress,
My unworthy life seems a miserable mess.
Handicapped, limited, with my strength
decreasing,
The demands on my time keep forever increasing.
And I pray for the flair and the force of youth
So I can keep spreading God's light and His truth,
For my heart's happy hope and my dearest
desire
Is to continue to serve You with fervor and fire,
But I no longer have strength to dramatically do
The spectacular things I loved doing for You,
Forgetting entirely that all You required
was not a servant the world admired
But a humbled heart and a sanctified soul
Whose only mission and purpose and goal
Was to be content with whatever God sends
And to know that to please You really depends
Not on continued and mounting success
But on learning how to become less and less
And to realize that we serve God best

When our one desire and only request
Is not to succumb to worldly acclaim
But to honor ourselves in Your holy name.
So let me say no to the flattery and praise
And quietly spend the rest of my days
Far from the greed and the speed of man,
Who has so distorted God's simple life plan.
And let me be great in the eyes of You, Lord,
For that is the richest, most priceless reward.

The greatest among you will be your
servant. For whover exalts himself will
be humbled, and whoever humbles
himself will be exalted.

~ Matthew 23:11-12 NIV ~

A special prayer for you

Oh blessed Father, hear this prayer
And keep all of us in Your care.
Give us patience and inner sight, too,
Just as You often used to do
When on the shores of the Galilee
You touched the blind and they could see
And cured the man who long was lame
When he but called Your holy name.
You are so great, we are so small,
And when trouble comes, as it does to us all,
There's so little that we can do
Except to place our trust in You.
So take the Savior's loving hand
And do not try to understand –
Just let Him lead you where He will,
Through pastures green and waters still,
And place yourself in His loving care,
And He will gladly help you bear
Whatever lies ahead of you,
And God will see you safely through –
And no earthly pain is ever too much
If God bestows His merciful touch.
So I commend you into His care

With a loving thought and a special prayer,
And always remember, whatever betide you,
God is always right beside you,
And you cannot go beyond His love and care,
For we are all a part of God, and God is every-
where.

A prescription

Just rest with quiet patience
and seek the Lord in prayer
And place yourself completely
in His ever-loving care,
Then do not fret or worry –
God will take good care of you,
For He's the Great Physician
and there's nothing He can't do.

Look to the Lord and his strength;
seek his face always. Remember the
wonders he has done, his miracles, and
the judgments he pronounced.

~ 1 Chronicles 16:11-12 NIV ~

A prayer for patience and comfort

Realizing my helplessness,
I'm asking God if He will bless
The thoughts you think and all you do
So these dark hours you're passing through
Will lose their grave anxiety
And only deep tranquillity
Will fill your mind and help impart
New strength and courage to your heart.

So place yourself in His loving care
And He will gladly help you bear
Whatever lies ahead of you,
For there is nothing God cannot do.
So I commend you into God's care,
And each day I will say a prayer
That you will feel His presence near
To help dissolve your every fear.

*Behold, God is my salvation; I will
trust, and will not be afraid, for the
Lord God is my strength and my song,
and he has become my salvation.*

~ Isaiah 12:2 RSV ~

God, grant me the glory of Thy gift

God, widen my vision so I may see
The afflictions You have sent to me
Not as a cross too heavy to wear
That weighs me down in gloomy despair,
Not as something to hate and despise
But a gift of love sent in disguise –
Something to draw me closer to You,
To teach me patience and forebearance, too,
Something to show me more clearly the way
To serve You and love You more every day,
Something priceless and precious and rare
That will keep me forever safe in Thy care,
Aware of the spiritual strength that is mine
If my selfish, small will is lost in Thine.

*For this slight momentary affliction is
preparing for us an eternal weight of
glory beyond all comparison.*

~ 2 Corinthians 4:17 RSV ~

Anxious prayers

When we are disturbed with a problem
and our minds are filled with doubt
And we struggle to find a solution
but there seems to be no way out,
We futilely keep on trying
to untangle our web of distress,
But our own little, puny efforts
meet with very little success.
And finally, exhausted and weary,
discouraged and downcast and low,
With no foreseeable answer
and with no other place to go,
We kneel down in sheer desperation
and slowly and stumblingly pray,
Then impatiently wait for an answer,
which we fully expect right away.
And then when God does not answer
in one sudden instant, we say,
"God does not seem to be listening,
so why should we bother to pray!"
But God can't get through to the anxious,
who are much too impatient to wait –
You have to believe in God's promise
that He comes not too soon or too late.
For whether God answers promptly

or delays in answering your prayer,
You must have faith to believe Him
and to know in you heart He'll be there.
So be not impatient or hasty –
just trust in the Lord and believe,
For whatever you ask in faith and love,
in abundance you are sure to receive.

For every one who asks receives ...

~ Luke 11:10 RSV ~

Prayers of thanks

*Rejoice always, never cease
praying, render constant thanks.*

~ 1 Thessalonians 5:16-18 NAB ~

Every day there are occasions to thank God
for the many blessings that He has showered
upon us: the gifts of nature, the gifts of love,
the gifts of food for our bodies and nourish-
ment for our souls and the greatest gift of all —
Jesus Christ, God's Son and the gift of life ever-
lasting.

So many reasons to love the Lord

Thank You, God, for little things
that come unexpectedly
To brighten up a dreary day
that dawned so dismally.
Thank You, God, for brushing
the dark clouds from my mind
And leaving only sunshine
and joy of heart behind.
Oh God, the list is endless
of things to thank You for,
But I take them all for granted
and unconsciously ignore
That everything I think or do,
each movement that I make,
Each measured, rhythmic heartbeat,
each breath of life I take
Is something You have given me
for which there is no way
For me in all my smallness
to in any way repay.

A thankful heart

Take nothing for granted,
for whenever you do,
The joy of enjoying
is lessened for you.
For we rob our own lives
much more than we know
When we fail to respond
or in any way show
Our thanks for the blessings
that daily are ours –
The warmth of the sun,
the fragrance of flowers,
The beauty of twilight,
the freshness of dawn,
The coolness of dew
on a green velvet lawn,
The kind little deeds
so thoughtfully done,
The favors of friends
and the love that someone
Unselfishly gives us
in a myriad of ways,
Expecting no payment
and no words of praise.
Oh, great is our loss

when we no longer find
A thankful response
to things of this kind.
For the joy of enjoying
and the fullness of living
Are found in the heart
that is filled with thanksgiving.

*Come into his presence
with thanksgiving.*

~ Psalm 95:2 RSV ~

Thanksgiving prayer

Thank You, God, for everything –
the big things and the small –
For every good gift comes from You,
the Giver of them all,
And all too often we accept
without any thanks or praise
The gifts You send as blessings
each day in many ways.
And so at this Thanksgiving time
we offer up a prayer
To thank You, God, for giving us
a lot more than our share.
First, thank You for the little things
that often come our way –
The things we take for granted
and don't mention when we pray –
The unexpected courtesy,
the thoughtful, kindly deed,
A hand reached out to help us
in the time of sudden need.
Oh, make us more aware, dear God,
of little daily graces
That come to us with sweet surprise
from never-dreamed-of places.
Then thank You for the miracles

we are much too blind too see,
And give us new awareness
of our many gifts from Thee.
And help us to remember
that the key to life and living
Is to make each prayer a prayer of thanks
and every day Thanksgiving.

*So then, just as you received Christ
Jesus as Lord, continue to live in him.*

~ Colossians 2:6 NIV ~

Praise and thanks to God

Touched by magic colors,
framed by velvet skies,
Nature's lovely masterpiece
serene, enchanting lies ...
I think this little haven
must be the kind of place
Where very unsuspectingly
we meet God face to face ...
For God is love and beauty,
and His gifts are peace and rest,
And in His soothing shelter
we are His welcome guests.

Praise the Lord from the heavens,
praise him in the heights! Praise him, all
his angels, praise him, all his host!
Praise him, sun and moon, praise him,
all you shining stars!

~ Psalm 148:1-3 RSV ~

Prayers of peace

"Blest too [are] the peacemakers."

~ Matthew 5:9 NAB ~

Peace is available to most, but achieved and accepted by too few. The seasons, location, wealth, and nationality are not the deciding factors; peace comes from within and is dependent upon your willingness to forgive, your capability to control bitterness, your ability to trust and to look beyond the present, and your adeptness for encouraging and possessing agape love.

A prayer for peace

O God, our help in ages past,
our hope in years to be,
Look down upon this troubled world
and see our need of Thee.
For in this age of unrest,
with violence all around,
We need Thy hand to lead us
to higher, safer ground.
Without Thy help and counsel
we are helpless to restore
Safety and security
in our hearts and homes once more.
And give us strength and courage
to be honorable and true
And to place our trust implicitly
in unseen things and You.
And keep us kind and humble
and fill our hearts with love,
Which in this selfish, greedy world
man has so little of,
Forgive us our transgressions
and help us find the way
To a better world for everyone
where man walks in peace each day.

We win by faith

Oh Father, grant once more to men
A simple, childlike faith again,
Forgetting color, race, or creed,
Seeing only the heart's deep need –
For faith alone can save man's soul
And make this torn world once more whole –
And faith in things we cannot see
Requires a child's simplicity.
And there is one unfailing course –
We win by faith and not by force.

*"Let the little children come to me,
and do not hinder them, for the
kingdom of God belongs to such
as these ... anyone who will not
receive the kingdom of God like
a little child will never enter it."*

~ Luke 18:16-17 NIV ~

The power of love

There is no thinking person
who can stand untouched today
And view the world around us
drifting downward to decay
Without feeling deep within him
a silent, unnamed dread,
Wondering how to stem the chaos
that lies frighteningly ahead.
But the problems we are facing
cannot humanly be solved,
For our diplomatic strategy
only gets us more involved,
And our skillful ingenuity,
our technology and science
Can never change a sinful heart
filled with hatred and defiance.
So our problems keep on growing
every hour of every day
As we vainly try to solve them
in our own self-willful way,
But man is powerless alone
to clean up the world outside
Until his own polluted soul
is clean and free inside.
For the amazing power of love

is beyond all comprehension,
And it alone can heal this world
of its hatred and dissension.

*Be imitators of God, therefore, as
dearly loved children and live a life of
love, just as Christ loved us and gave
himself up for us as a fragrant offering
and sacrifice to God.*

~ Ephesians 5:1-2 NIV ~

Keep our nation
in Thy care

We are faced with many problems
that grow bigger day by day,
And as we seek to solve them
in our self-sufficient way,
We keep drifting into chaos,
and our avarice and greed
Blind us to the answer
that would help us meet our need.
Oh God, renew our spirits
and make us more aware
That our future is dependent
on sacrifice and prayer.
Forgive us our transgressions
and revive our faith anew,
So we may all draw closer
to each other and to You.
For when a nation is too proud
to kneel and daily pray,
It will crumble into chaos
and descend into decay.
So stir us with compassion
and raise our standards higher,
And take away our lust for power

and make our one desire
To be a shining symbol
of all that's great and good
As you lead us in our struggle
toward new-found brotherhood.

*If my people, who are called by my
name, will humble themselves and pray
and seek my face and turn from their
wicked ways, then will I hear from
heaven and will forgive their sin and
will heal their land.*

~ 2 Chronicles 7:14 NIV ~

A prayer in conclusion

Accept our thanks, Heavenly Father,
For giving meaning to why we pray,
For granting patience as we live
Through each and every day,
For adding power through Your presence
We ask that it never cease.
Help us to be ever grateful
As we strive for inner peace.

V.J.R.